Which Switch is Which?
A first look at electricity

Sam Godwin

an imprint of Hodder Children's Books

UNIVERSITY OF CENTRAL ENGLAND LIBRARY SERVICES

It is night-time. All is quiet and still.

Come on, let's find something to eat.

7

It is difficult to see in the dark.

Sssh! You're going to wake everyone up!

8

9

So we turn on the lights.

I'll turn on this switch – three cheers for electricity!

Electricity comes from a power station.

It flows along wires and into our homes.

So, the wires must come in through a hole in the wall!

Other wires carry the electricity around the home,

Mummy, where are the wires for this switch?

Sometimes, wires are hidden inside a wall.

14

15

And more wires carry the electricity

That silly moth keeps flying towards the light.

from the switches to the lights.

I can't help it.
It's so pretty.
Ouch!

Electricity not only gives us light.

It makes things move...

What's this, Mummy?

It's a plug. Plugs connect things to the switches.

This washing machine uses electricity, too.

22

... it makes sound...

23

25

26

All about electricity

When it's dark, we need electric light to be able to see clearly.

Electricity travels into our homes along wires. The wires are connected to switches around the home.

Pressing a switch turns a light on.

Pressing a switch turns a light off.